Cars and Trucks

Philip Steele

CRESTWOOD HOUSE
New York

Horsepower!

Who invented the wheel?
Nobody really knows.
Wheeled vehicles were in
use in the Middle East
by about 5,000 years ago.
Carts and wagons had to
be pulled by animals such
as horses or oxen. When
engines were first
invented, people measured
the work they could do in
"horsepower."

The horseless carriage

For hundreds of years, people tried to invent vehicles that did not
rely on horses. They came up with some strange ideas. Many inventions
could only work on smooth surfaces, and roads were very rough in those
days. The carriage below was built by a French engineer named Nicolas
Cugnot in 1769. It was designed for pulling guns into battle. It worked
on steam produced by a large boiler at the front. It was clumsy and was
easily overturned. Its top speed was barely 1.8 miles per hour.

Cugnot steam carriage 1769-70

The first gas-driven cars

People started using steam wagons to haul loads. Engineers tried to make lighter engines for cars. In 1885, a German engineer named Karl Benz built a light car with a gasoline engine. It had three wheels and seated two people. It traveled at 7.8 mph. The car was built on a frame of steel tubes.

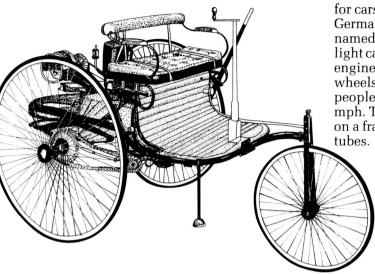

Benz 3-wheeler
1885-86

On the road

By the end of the last century, the first cars could be seen on the roads. They were rare and expensive and often broke down. Tires were made of solid rubber.

Fiat 1899

3

The trail-blazers

Automobile design improved year by year. Pneumatic tires, using air-filled inner tubes, replaced solid rubber tires. Better roads were built. Some car makes became famous as touring cars. Others were stars of the race circuits. Car racing began in 1895.

Cadillac 1903 The US became one of the world's great automobile producers.

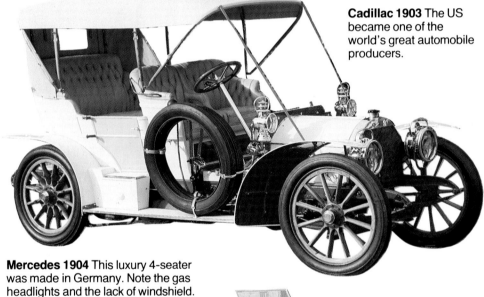

Mercedes 1904 This luxury 4-seater was made in Germany. Note the gas headlights and the lack of windshield.

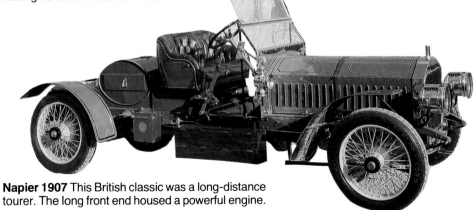

Napier 1907 This British classic was a long-distance tourer. The long front end housed a powerful engine.

Motoring for all

Ford Model T 1908 More than 15 million Model Ts were sold between 1908 and 1927. In 1908, the car cost $850. Eight years later, it cost only $360.

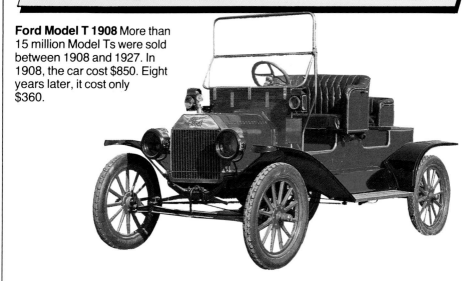

The first cars were built by hand, one by one. An American named Henry Ford decided to build cars on a production line. This meant that cars could be mass-produced by teams of factory workers. Each worker on the line did one special job. More cars could be produced this way — and for less money. Ordinary people were then able to afford them. By 1926 Ford, based in Detroit, Michigan, had become the world's largest car manufacturer. Ford cars were reliable and easy to drive.

Ford Thunderbird 1955 By the 1950s, Ford's designs had become streamlined. Cars were long and sleek, with rounded hoods and tail fins.

5

How does an engine work?

The gasoline engine is an internal-combustion engine. This means that fuels are burned inside it to provide power. The engine is made of a solid block of metal bored with holes called cylinders. Gasoline from the tank is mixed with air in a device called the carburetor. The mixture is fed into the cylinders through inlets called valves. A sliding rod called a piston rises up the cylinder and squeezes, or compresses, the mixture. Spark plugs light the mixture, causing an explosion. The force of this drives the piston down. Leftover fumes (exhaust) escape through the valve outlets. The pistons are connected by rods to the crankshaft. As they move up and down inside the cylinders, they turn the crankshaft around. This motion powers the wheels. The crankshaft also powers the camshaft, which opens and closes the valves.

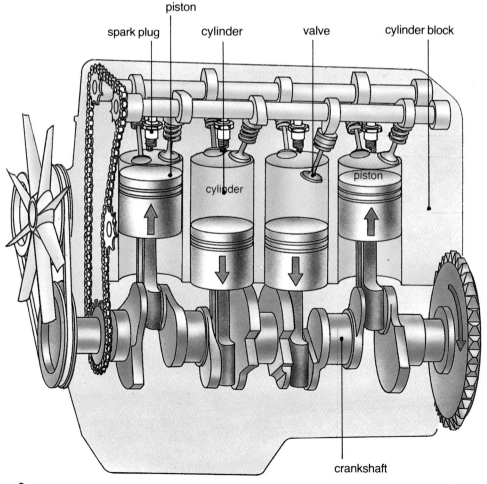

piston

spark plug   cylinder   valve   cylinder block

cylinder

piston

crankshaft

How do the pistons work?

The series of piston movements that take place in the cylinder are called strokes. Cars normally use a four-stroke engine. The four strokes can be seen below. Each cylinder explosion turns the crankshaft halfway around. The cylinders fire in a very rapid sequence.

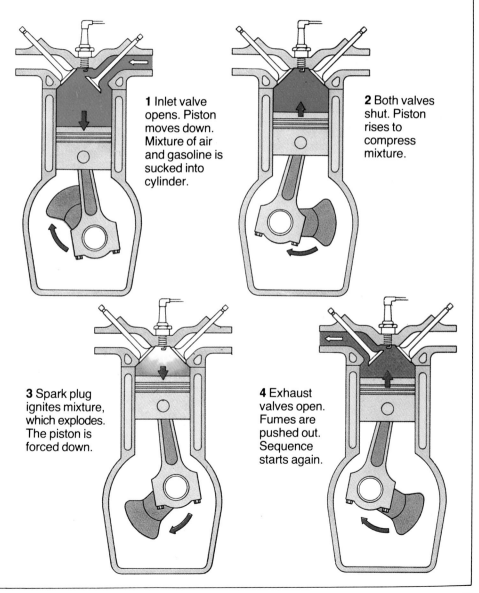

1 Inlet valve opens. Piston moves down. Mixture of air and gasoline is sucked into cylinder.

2 Both valves shut. Piston rises to compress mixture.

3 Spark plug ignites mixture, which explodes. The piston is forced down.

4 Exhaust valves open. Fumes are pushed out. Sequence starts again.

What is a diesel engine?

Inventors in the 19th century designed internal-combustion engines that ran on other fuels than gasoline. Diesel fuel is thicker than gasoline. It is used in a kind of engine first developed by Rudolf Diesel in 1892.

Diesel engines do not use spark plugs and do not need a mixture of fuel and air. Instead, air alone is taken into the cylinder. It is compressed far more than the mixture in a gasoline engine. As the air is squeezed, it becomes hotter and hotter, reaching a temperature of between 2357 and 3000°F. Then, diesel fuel is injected into the cylinder or into a special combustion chamber.

As the drops of fuel spray in, they mix with the air and ignite. The explosion forces the piston down the cylinder. This turns the crankshaft. Diesel engines may be designed to work on a two-stroke or a four-stroke system.

Diesel engines are used for many kinds of transport. Most trucks and some cars and taxis use diesel fuel. It is cheaper than gasoline and does more work gallon for gallon. However, diesel engines are noisier and smellier than gasoline engines.

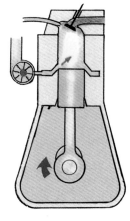

1 The piston is down. Air is blown into the cylinder through a valve.

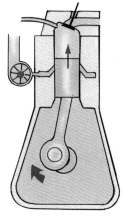

2 The piston rises. The air is compressed and becomes very hot.

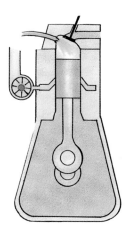

3 A jet of diesel fuel is sprayed into the hot air inside.

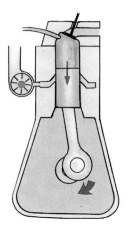

4 The fuel mixes with the hot air and explodes. The piston moves down.

How do gears work?

Gears are machines that are designed to transfer motion. Toothed wheels inside the transmission transfer motion from the crankshaft to the drive shaft. These gears control the speed at which the drive shaft turns and its direction.

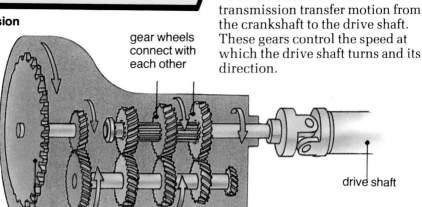

transmission

gear wheels connect with each other

drive shaft

flywheel helps engine run smoothly

What turns the wheels?

The power may be transferred from the transmission either to the rear wheels, or to the front wheels, or to all four wheels. In rear-wheel drive, the drive shaft is linked to the back axle, the shaft that joins the rear wheels. The axle includes two half-shafts which are controlled by a system of gears called the differential. These gears change the direction of drive.

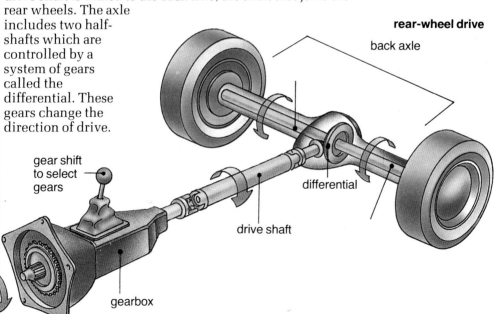

rear-wheel drive

back axle

gear shift to select gears

differential

drive shaft

gearbox

How do brakes work?

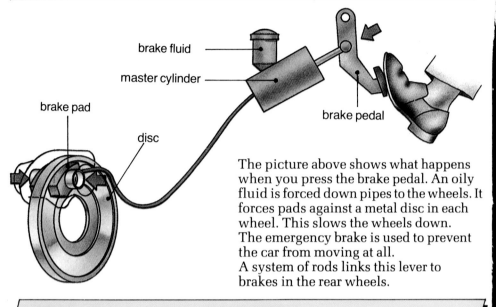

brake fluid

master cylinder

brake pad

disc

brake pedal

The picture above shows what happens when you press the brake pedal. An oily fluid is forced down pipes to the wheels. It forces pads against a metal disc in each wheel. This slows the wheels down. The emergency brake is used to prevent the car from moving at all. A system of rods links this lever to brakes in the rear wheels.

How are cars steered?

When the steering wheel is turned, it turns the steering column. A gear wheel called a pinion meshes with a toothed bar called a rack. As the pinion turns, it moves the rack to the left or right. Track rods turn the front wheels as required to change the car's direction.

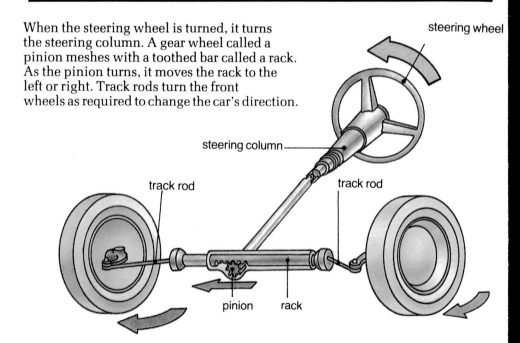

steering wheel

steering column

track rod

track rod

pinion   rack

Holding the road

As the wheels spin along the road surface, the vehicle must be cushioned against bumps and ruts. A series of springs and shock absorbers make up the suspension system. This and air-filled tires ensure a smooth ride. The tires rub against the road surface as they spin. This force is called friction. Another force, called traction, presses the tires against the road. Ice or water reduce these forces, so the car may skid. Grip is improved by the tread, a pattern of grooves in the tire rubber. Different vehicles need different treads.

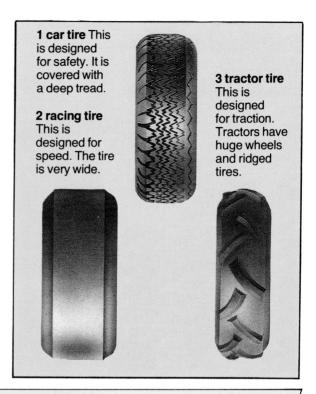

1 car tire This is designed for safety. It is covered with a deep tread.

2 racing tire This is designed for speed. The tire is very wide.

3 tractor tire This is designed for traction. Tractors have huge wheels and ridged tires.

Riding with the wind

The shape of a car is not merely a question of fashion. It affects the way the car moves and holds the road. This Porsche 911 is built for speed. It has wide tires to grip the road surface. It has a low, streamlined appearance so that the air flows over it easily. At the rear it has a "spoiler." This shape interrupts the air flow, so that the wheels are forced downward to grip the road surface.

Who designs cars?

Car design involves many branches of science, from mechanics to chemistry and electronics. All the big car manufacturers have researchers and designers who try out new ideas on computers. They can see how these ideas apply to the ways in which cars are used every day. Sometimes racing car technology is adapted for use in other types of cars. Designers work on ideas for economy cars and for luxury cars. They make sure that the cars use the smallest amount of fuel necessary. They make sure they are safe. Some cars have built-in computer systems. Your own car reminds you to fasten your seat belt!

A framework of steel

Modern car design combines lightweight materials with tough metals. The car on the right is built around a framework of steel. If the car crashes, the front or rear crumples and takes the shock. The passengers are safe inside a shell of super-tough steel. An overhead bar protects them in case the car turns over.

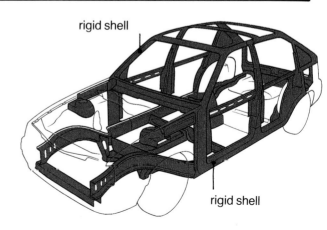

rigid shell

rigid shell

Where are cars made?

Large automobile firms have factories in many countries. Different factories may build different parts of the same car. The cars are then assembled on a production line. Firms may use robots to do much of the work.

Safety first

New cars are tested in every way possible. Here a test model has been made to crash. The dummies show that real people would have been safe in the crash if they had been wearing their seat belts.

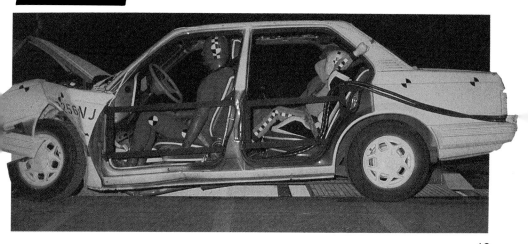

Built for speed

Driving has changed a lot in the last 30 years. High-speed expressways now link cities in many parts of the world. Sports cars like this German Porsche 911 can travel long distances very quickly. Sports cars are exciting to drive. However, they are expensive and use a lot of fuel.

The family car

The Citroën BX is a French sedan. Family cars need four doors and often have a fifth as a "hatchback." Speed is less important than reliability. Family cars need lots of room for passengers and trunk space for luggage or packages. Some cars have body panels made of plastic. These make the car lighter and are easy to repair.

A lead-free future

The car below is an English Vauxhall. It is a family car with five speeds. There are four different engine sizes, with top speeds ranging from 105 to 125 mph. The 1.4 model can cover 50 miles per gallon of gas used, when traveling at 54 mph. A switch converts the car to use lead-free gasoline. Gasoline with lead in it poisons the air we breathe. The cars of the future should be safer and cleaner.

Highway driving

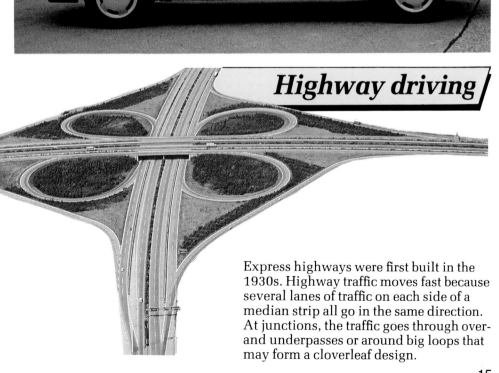

Express highways were first built in the 1930s. Highway traffic moves fast because several lanes of traffic on each side of a median strip all go in the same direction. At junctions, the traffic goes through over- and underpasses or around big loops that may form a cloverleaf design.

On the streets

Not all driving takes place on highways. City streets are crowded and traffic jams may build up. Exhaust fumes contain dangerous substances such as lead which pollute the air. Most cars are now designed to use lead-free gasoline. Sometimes traffic is kept out of downtown areas. Computer-controlled traffic lights help regulate traffic flow.

Cars for the city

Cars used in cities should use little gasoline and be inexpensive to run. There is little point in having an expensive car using up gallons of fuel in a traffic jam. The cars should be small so that they can be parked easily. Many such cars have been designed in Europe by firms such as Fiat, Renault and Volkswagen. One of the most popular British cars of the 1960s was the Mini Minor. It was followed by the successful Mini Metro.

Mini Metro

The luxury car

Some cars have large engines that use a lot of gasoline. These cars are fine pieces of engineering and are very comfortable. Often people enjoy driving around in a Cadillac or a Rolls-Royce. Sometimes especially large and luxurious cars are called limousines.

Cadillac Fleetwood Brougham

A car for the 90s

The Jaguar XJ-S is a British luxury sports car that was introduced in 1988. This model is a convertible. At the push of a button, its roof slides back for warm-weather driving. It can accelerate from 0-58 mph in 7.9 seconds and has a top speed of 145 mph.

Grand Prix

Racing cars are divided into classes, depending on the size of the car and engine. Top class cars belong to Formula 1. They race in a series of international competitions known as "Grand Prix" events. Average speeds can exceed 140 mph.

Pit stop!

Today's racetracks are specially designed for incredibly high speeds. Repairs and refueling are carried out in a race during pit stops. Trained teams refuel cars, change tires and carry out repairs at lightning speed. The fastest pit stop on record took place during the famous Indianapolis 500, when a car was refueled in just four seconds!

The dragsters

In drag racing, cars are timed over a short distance. The vehicles are very light, but they are powered by massive engines. At the start, friction heats the tires until they smoke. Some dragsters have piston engines that use special fuels. Some have jet or rocket engines.

Special vehicle races

If it moves, you can race it! Not all tracks are for Formula 1 vehicles. Cars of all types and ages can be adapted for use on the track. The body can be altered, the engine changed and racing tires added. Even trucks and public transportation vehicles can be rebuilt for racing. Sometimes old cars are driven so they collide into each other and smash! These stock cars are racing at the Spedeworth Lynden Race Track, in England.

Off the beaten track

Vehicles have to be designed for all kinds of conditions. Beyond the network of roads and highways lie some real challenges. Vehicles have been designed to travel through deserts, mountains, and jungles. These cars must withstand extreme heat, cold, and dampness as well as mud, snow, and sand. They need to carry spare parts and extra fuel.

Cross-country vehicles

This Land Rover is being used by photographers on safari in Kenya. It has to cover rough bush country where there are no paved roads. It has extra gears and four-wheel drive. It has tires with heavy treads. No one wants to break down when there are hungry lions around!

Electric buggies

This rent-a-buggy is in Amsterdam, in the Netherlands. It runs along special routes in the city center, helping reduce the number of private cars.

It runs on electricity, which is cheaper than gasoline and does not pollute the air.

Electric vehicles have been in use for many years as delivery vans. They use batteries that must be recharged, and cannot provide enough power for high-speed travel. In recent years, electric cars have been developed that are much more efficient. One day we may all be driving with battery power!

Out of this world

One of the most famous cars ever built was driven across the surface of the moon during the Apollo 15 mission of 1971. The LRV (Lunar Roving Vehicle) carried two astronauts and covered 17 miles. Powered by batteries, it weighed 470 lbs. and could reach a top speed of 10 mph.

Working giants

Trucks are sometimes articulated. This means that they have two parts. The front, or "tractor," unit pulls the trailer, which carries the load.

Peterbilt (USA)

The road train

This "road train" is carrying cattle across the Australian outback. In remote parts of Australia, many trucks haul a series of trailers. In countries with busier roads, only single or sometimes double trailers are allowed.

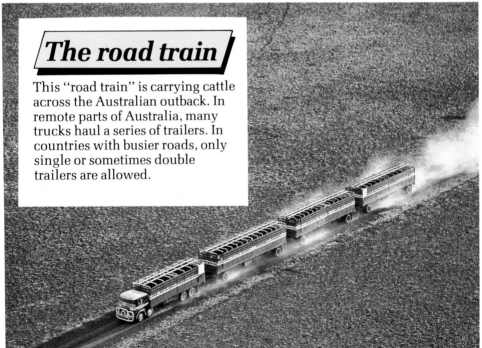

Push and pull power

Trucks are not used only for hauling. The ones on the left have been fitted with snow-plows. They are clearing snow-drifts from an airport runway. The same airport will use all kinds of special vehicles, such as fire engines, ambulances, security vans, police vans, tractors for towing aircraft, delivery vans, garbage trucks and runway sweepers.

Many other industries have trucks specially designed for their own needs. The largest of all are used in mining and quarrying. Their huge wheels tower over a human being. Trucks have powerful diesel engines. Many have double sets of heavy-duty tires to provide as much traction as possible. Long-distance trucks often have compartments for drivers to sleep in.

Lifting and Loading

The truck on the right is raising access stairs up to a cargo plane.

Many trucks have sections that can lift up goods on board or dump loads such as soil or garbage out the back. The lifting power comes from piped fluids, or hydraulics.

Carrying bulk

This American truck is designed to carry heavy loads of loose, bulky material such as sand or soil. Dump trucks have strong open trailers on the back, which can be tipped by hydraulics. Dumpsters have back trailers that can be removed by hoists. The biggest dump truck in the world is American. It can carry a load of over 330 tons.

Carrying liquid

Tank trucks are designed to carry liquids or gases. The tank truck below provides water in the desert. The plants being watered will stop sand from blowing across the highway. Tanker loads include milk, gasoline and oil. Drivers carrying dangerous loads such as chemicals must have a warning sign on their vehicles.

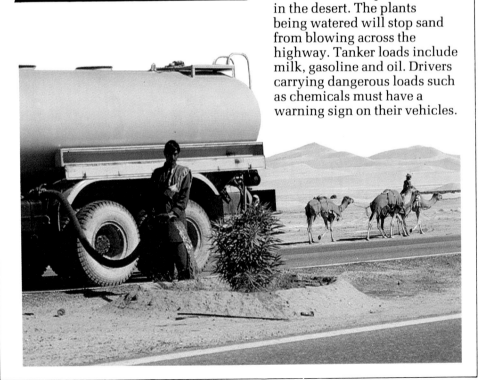

The lumberjacks

This articulated truck has been designed to carry huge tree trunks from a lumber camp to a sawmill. It has a long-bodied open trailer with support rails along the sides. Many timber trailers have hydraulic hoists for loading and unloading the timber. This tractor unit is American built.

Trucks and freight

Trucks line the dock at Port Harcourt, Nigeria. Basic trucks like these are used in every part of the world. They can carry freight of all shapes and sizes, from sacks to boxes. Tarpaulins protect the goods in transit.

The container trade

Today, most articulated trucks can carry containers on their trailers. These are metal boxes of a standard size. They can be stacked easily, and transferred to ship or train as required. Containers are rigid, so they protect the goods inside them. They are easily sealed.

Trucks and passengers

In many parts of the world, there are few buses or trains. Trucks form the main long-distance traffic. Trucks may carry many passengers, who pay the driver for the ride.

Transporting vehicles

Vehicles themselves must be transported from time to time. Large trucks may carry vehicles such as earth-moving equipment that can only move slowly. New cars may be transported on a double-decker truck. This allows six or seven cars to be delivered at a time. Emergency vehicles may be flown to the scene of a disaster in a large cargo plane so that they arrive without delay.

In the picture on the left, the trailer of a large milk tanker is being unloaded from a ship in Miami, Florida.

Roll on, roll off

Loading and unloading vehicles from a ship is difficult. This ferry (right) is called a "ro-ro," or "**ro**ll on, **ro**ll off." The ship can open up to allow cars and trucks to drive on. At the other end, the cars and trucks simply drive off.

The record breakers

★ The biggest car ever was specially built in the United States. It was a 60-foot-long Cadillac. It had 16 wheels and a swimming pool!

★ The first car with four wheels was built by German engineer Gottlieb Daimler in 1885.

★ The first pneumatic, or air-filled, tires were designed by E. and A. Michelin of France in 1895.

★ The car series produced over the longest time is the Volkswagen "Beetle," which first appeared 50 years ago.

★ The largest car factory in the world is the Volkswagen works at Wolfsburg in West Germany.

A century of speed

	mph	60	120	180	240
1885 Benz 3-wheeler Germany	Karl Benz				
1899 La Jamais Contente France	Camille Jenatzy				
1904 Gobron Brillie France		Louis Rigolly			
1927 Sunbeam Britain				Henry Seagrove	
1947 Napier-Railton Britain					
1964 Spirit of America USA					
1970 The Blue Flame USA					
1983 Thrust 2 Britain					

★ The official world land-speed record is held by British racer Richard Noble. His vehicle, *Thrust 2*, had a Rolls-Royce jet engine. It traveled at 610 mph across the Nevada desert. The official record for a rocket-engined vehicle stands at 600 mph, although unofficially it is said that one has topped Noble's record.

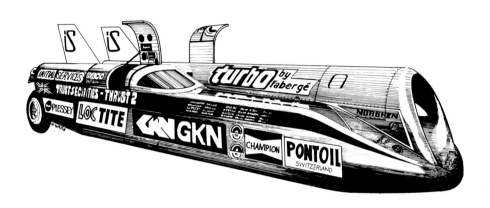

360	420	480	540	600

John Cobb

Craig Breedlove

Gary Gabelich

Richard Noble

Index

The numbers in **bold** are illustrations.

Originally published by Macmillan Children's Books, a division of Macmillan Publishers, Ltd. Subsequently published by Heinemann Children's Reference, a division of Heinemann Educational Books Ltd., Halley Court, Jordan Hill, Oxford OX2 8EJ. Companies and representatives throughout the world.

CRESTWOOD HOUSE

Macmillan Publishing Company
866 Third Avenue
New York, NY 10022

Collier Macmillan Canada, Inc.
1200 Eglinton Avenue East
Suite 200
Don Mills, Ontario M3C 3N1

First Edition

10 9 8 7 6 5 4 3 2 1

Design by Julian Holland Publishing Ltd

Steele, Philip.
    Cars and trucks / by Philip Steele — 1st U.S. ed.
         p.   cm. — (Pocket facts)
     Includes index.
     Summary: Discusses many aspects of cars and trucks, including their history, different kinds, how they are designed and built, and how they work.
      ISBN 0-89686-521-5
      1. Automobiles — Juvenile literature. 2. Trucks — Juvenile literature. [1. Automobiles. 2. Trucks.] I. Title. II. Series: Pocket facts (New York, N.Y.)
TL147.SL34   1991
629.222 — dc20

90 – 41180
CIP
AC

Acknowledgments

Cover: Photo Researchers, Inc.: Ray Ellis
Illustrations: BLA Publishing Ltd, Nigel White;
Photographs: *a = above, m = middle, b = below*
3*b*, 4*a*, 4*m*, 4*b*, 5*a*, 5*b* The National Motor Museum, Beaulieu; 11*b* Porsche Cars; 12*a* Hank Morgan/Science Photo Library; 13*b* Cincinnati Milacron; 14*a* ZEFA; 14*m* Porsche Cars; 14*b* Loek Polders; 15*a* Vauxhall Motors; 15*b* Loek Polders; 16*a* ZEFA; 16*m* Austin Rover; 17*a* General Motors (Cadillac); 17*b* Jaguar Cars Ltd; 18*a*, 18*b* L.A.T. Photographic; 19*a* ZEFA; 19*b* Barnaby's Picture Library; 20*a* Stephen Krasemann/ NHPA; 20*b* Jonathan Scott/Seaphot; 21*a* Loek Polders; 21*b* ZEFA; 22*a* The National Motor Museum, Beaulieu; 22*b* ZEFA; 23*a*, 23*b* British Airports Authority; 24*a*, 24*b*, 25*a* ZEFA; 25*b* Robert Harding Picture Library; 26*a*, 26*b*, 27*a* ZEFA; 27*b* ZEFA.